ARGENTINA

A TRUE BOOK

by

Michael Burgan

Children's Press®

A Division of Grolier Publishing

New York London Hong Kong Sydney
Danbury, Connecticut

Reading Consultant
Linda Cornwell
Learning Resource Consultant
Indiana Department of
Education

An Argentine
sunflower field

**Visit Children's Press® on the
Internet at:
http://publishing.grolier.com**

Library of Congress Cataloging-in-Publication Data

Burgan, Michael.
    Argentina / by Michael Burgan.
      p.   cm.—(A true book)
    Includes bibliographical references and index.
    Summary: Presents an overview of the history, geography, and culture
of Argentina.
    ISBN: 0-516-21188-9 (lib.bdg.)   0-516-26490-7(pbk.)
    1.   Argentina—Juvenile literature. [1. Argentina.] I. Title. II. Series.
F2808.2.B87 1999
982—dc21   98-2813
                                               CIP
                                               AC

GROLIER
PUBLISHING   2 3 4 5 6 7 8 9 10 R 08 07 06 05 04 03 02

Contents

BOLIVIA

BRAZIL

PARAGUAY

CHILE

N
W   E
S

Jujuy

Salta

Formosa

GRAN CHACO

Santiago del Estero

Catamarca

Corrientes

Porto Alegre

La Rioja

San Juan

Cordoba

MESOPOTAMIA

Mendoza

San Luis

URUGUAY

Buenos Aires ★

★

Montevideo

Santa Rosa

PAMPA

ANDES MOUNTAINS

Neuquén

PACIFIC OCEAN

ATLANTIC OCEAN

ARGENTINA

Rawson

PATAGONIA

ARGENTINA

Falkland
Islands

Río Gallegos

Strait of Magellan

0   200 miles

Tierra del Fuego

0   300 kilometers

A Large Land

Argentina is a country on the east coast of South America. It is the second-largest country in South America. Argentina stretches almost 2,300 miles (3,700 kilometers) from north to south. At its widest point, the country is about 980 miles (1,577 km) across.

The Andes Mountains stretch along Argentina's western border. Just beyond the Andes lies the country of Chile. Argentina's other neighbors are Bolivia and Paraguay to the north, and Brazil and Uruguay to the east. *Argentina* means "silvery land" in Spanish. The Spaniards who first settled in Argentina hoped to find large amounts of silver there.

The Iguaçu Falls are a favorite tourist attraction in Argentina.

The tallest mountain in North and South America lies within Argentina. This peak, Mount Aconcagua, is 22,831 feet (6,959 meters) high. Another natural wonder is Iguaçu Falls, between Argentina and Brazil. Its rushing waters are more than 2 miles (3.2 km) wide!

The people of Argentina live and work in three major regions. In the north is the Gran Chaco, a mixture of grassy plains and pine forests. The fertile, flat lands of the Pampa make up the central region of Argentina. Most Argentines make the Pampa their home.

A cattle rancher in the
Pampa region

The icy waters of Patagonia

The largest and southern-most region of Argentina is Patagonia. It is a dry and windy plateau, with rocky cliffs and canyons.

Argentina's Wildlife

Chilean flamingos

Argentina has a great variety of wildlife. Flamingos live in the warm, humid north, and penguins gather on the cold southern tip of Argentina.

In the central region, there are fierce wild cats and many types of reptiles. Argentina is also the home to the flightless, ostrich-like rhea. Some farmers raise these birds and offer rhea rides to children!

Jaguar

The flightless rhea

The People of Argentina

More than 35 million people live in Argentina. Its citizens are called Argentines. Nine out of ten Argentines live in cities or large towns. The biggest city is Buenos Aires, the country's capital. More than 12 million people live in or near this modern city.

An aerial view of Buenos Aires, Argentina's capital

The first Europeans came to Argentina in 1516. These early settlers were Spanish. When they reached the Pampa, they found the land occupied by South American Indians. Most of the Indians eventually died from diseases brought by the Europeans. Today, about forty thousand Indians live in Argentina. Most of them are *mestizos*, people with both Indian and European ancestors.

Spain controlled Argentina for hundreds of years, but other Europeans also came to live there. People from Germany, Wales, and England came to farm. Then, in the late 1800s, Italians arrived by the thousands. Many worked hard in construction jobs. Today, Italians are the largest ethnic group in Argentina.

Smaller numbers of settlers came to Argentina from the

A Roman Catholic church in Argentina

Middle East and Asia. And some Africans were forced to come as slaves.

Wherever they came from, the new Argentines learned Spanish, the country's official language. Many of them joined the Roman Catholic Church. Today, nine out of ten Argentines follow that religion.

Building a Nation

In the early 1500s, the South American Indians of Argentina were mostly nomads—people who roamed across the Pampas with herds of animals. The nomads clashed with the Spaniards who tried to settle on their lands. Many of the nomads were forced off their own land

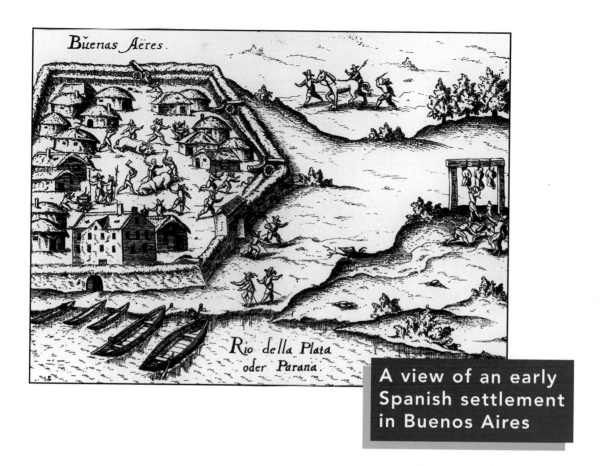

Buenas Aeres.

Rio della Plata
oder Parana.

A view of an early
Spanish settlement
in Buenos Aires

in search of new homes. By the
1600s, Spain had set up towns
along the borders of Argentina.
Slowly, the Spaniards took control of the whole country.

In the early 1800s, many Argentines wanted to run their own country. But others were loyal to Spain. The two sides argued and sometimes fought bloody battles. Finally, on July 9, 1816, Argentina became an independent nation, but the fighting did not end.

Many rich landowners, called *caudillos*, raised armies and fought one another for control of the new country. In 1829, a wealthy citizen of

Argentina took complete control. His name was Juan Manuel de Rosas, and he ruled as a dictator until 1852.

Many Argentines disliked de Rosas, so they rebelled against him. The people then set up a government similar to the system used in the United States. They had a president, and a congress made the country's laws.

After 1853, Argentina became more modern. Wealthy

Farming (above) and the construction of railroads (opposite page) led to Argentina's rapid growth.

people from England helped build the country's railroads, and immigrants from Europe set up farms. Entering the

1900s, Argentina was one of South America's richest nations, but the country remained without political harmony.

The Gauchos of the Pampa

Gauchos are the cowboys of Argentina. In the 1800s, gauchos were skilled and rugged horsemen who rode across the wide Pampa, searching for wild cattle or working on ranches. Most gauchos wore wide-brimmed hats and baggy pants called *bombachas*. When they went hunting, gauchos twirled a *boleadora*. This weapon has three stones on a leather strap and is thrown at a target. Only a few gauchos remain today, but many stories and songs continue to honor their memory.

A boleadora

Years of Troubles

In 1930, many Argentines were out of work, and the government was corrupt. A group of army generals decided to take control of the country. These men helped to create new jobs, but they also limited the people's freedom.

President Juan Perón (standing, left) and his wife Eva celebrate his inauguration in 1952.

In 1944, an army colonel named Juan D. Perón was one of Argentina's leaders. He supported the country's workers and tried to raise their wages. Perón became very popular, and in 1946 he was elected president. Perón's wife, Eva, had been an actress, and the people grew to love her. Her popularity helped Perón win another election in 1952, but Eva Perón died that same year.

After the death of his wife, Perón continued to improve life for the average Argentines. He also gave women the right to vote. But many of his programs cost millions of dollars to run, and by 1955 Argentina could not afford them. Once again, the military took control, forcing Perón from power.

For almost twenty years, Argentina had military rulers. Then Perón briefly returned to

After Juan Perón's death in 1974, his wife Isabel was president until 1976.

power in 1973. When he died, his new wife, Isabel, became president. She was the first woman to lead a South American country. In 1976,

Argentina's brutal army generals took control again, killing thousands of people who opposed them. These killings are known as the "Dirty War." Many of their victims have never been found.

By 1982, military leaders were at war with Britain. Argentina claimed it owned the Falkland Islands, which are near the southern tip of the country. (Argentines call them the Malvinas.) Britain had

West Point Island, Falkland Islands

ruled there for more than 150 years. Argentina lost that war, and its military rulers gave up their power. In 1983, democracy and greater freedom returned to Argentina.

Work in Argentina

Argentina is one of the most modern countries in South America. It makes many industrial goods, such as cars and appliances. Most of these are sold within the country. One of every five workers helps to make these kinds of products. To power its plants, Argentina

Some of the many products manufactured in Argentina are oil (top) and automobiles (bottom).

relies on oil and natural gas. Unlike most countries, Argentina produces its own oil, which also provides jobs for the people.

More than half of the country's workers are in the service industry. They work in stores, banks, hospitals, and in government. The most important part of the Argentine economy is farming. Farmers grow wheat, corn, and other grains on the rich soil of the Pampas.

The Pampa produces about two-thirds of the nation's agricultural output on its rich soil.

Fresh grapes are one of Argentina's leading exports.

They export (sell to other countries) most of these crops. Argentina is one of the world's leaders in growing wheat. The country also has vast fruit orchards, and its vineyards grow grapes for wine.

Some of Argentina's plentiful grain is used to feed cattle and sheep raised on large ranches. The ranchers own more than fifty million cattle. The beef from this cattle is another major export. Many factories make food products that are sold around the world.

Tango and Tea

When they are not working, Argentines relax in many ways. They enjoy sports—especially soccer—as well as movies and theater. Two things have a special place in the country's culture—*yerba maté* and the tango.

Yerba maté, a type of tea, is the national drink of Argentina.

Yerba maté is a favorite of the gauchos.

Today, across the country, people get together to share a relaxing moment with yerba maté.

To make the tea, leaves are placed in a special wooden cup, called a *maté*. Hot water is then poured over the leaves. After a few minutes, the tea is ready. People drink yerba maté through a silver straw called a *bombilla*. A group of people may share the same drink, taking turns sipping though the straw.

Yerba maté is not well known outside of South America, but another Argentine specialty is

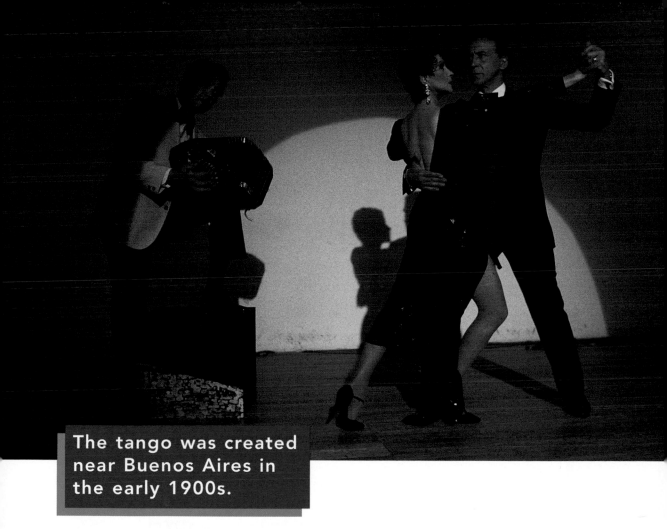

The tango was created near Buenos Aires in the early 1900s.

famous around the world—the tango. The tango is a kind of music created in Argentina in the early 1900s. The tunes are usually slow, and the words to these songs often talk about the sorrows of life.

The tango is also a famous dance performed to this music. The tango was popular in the 1920s, and it is still danced today.

The Argentines are proud of their tea, their tango, and their country. They have blended the cultures of many different peoples to create a unique land.

The annual gaucho festival
in San Antonio de Areco

To Find Out More

Here are some additional resources to help you learn more about the nation of Argentina.

 **Books**

Brusca, Maria Christina. **On the Pampas.** Henry Holt, 1991.

Fox, Geoffrey. **The Land and People of Argentina.** J.B. Lippincott, 1990.

Lerner Geography Department. **Argentina in Pictures.** Lerner Publications, 1988.

Petersen, David. **South America.** Children's Press, 1998.

Peterson, Marge and Bob. **Argentina: A Wild West Heritage.** Dillon, 1990.

Organizations and Online Sites

Argentina
http://middlebury.edu/ ~leparc/htm/argent2.htm

A general overview of Argentine history and the country today, with pictures.

Embassy of the Argentine Republic
1600 New Hampshire Avenue, N.W. Washington, D.C. 20009

Information About Yerba Maté
http://reality.sgi.com/ employees/omar/personal/ Argentina/mate.html

This site provides more details about yerba maté, Argentina's national drink, with links to other sites.

La Patagonia
http://www.lapatagonia.com

The history and sights of Argentina's rugged Patagonia region.

Piazzolla.Org
http://www.piazzolla.org

A site dedicated to Astor Piazzolla, Argentina's modern master of the tango. You can learn more about the music and hear some of Piazzolla's recordings.

United Nations Information Center
1775 K Street, N.W. Washington, D.C. 20008

Important Words

ancestors relatives who lived long
   ago

corrupt doing bad or illegal things

culture the customs and beliefs of a
   group of people

dictator ruler who has complete control over a country

ethnic a person's racial or national
   background

exports materials and products sold
   to other countries

fertile able to grow many crops

nomads people who move from one
   place to another to live

Index

Meet the Author

Michael Burgan lives in Hartford, Connecticut. A former editor for *Weekly Reader*, he now writes for both young people and adults.

Mr. Burgan has written more than fifteen books, including original stories for children. His educational books include a biography of U.S. Secretary of State Madeleine Albright and a series on disasters.

Michael has a B.A. degree in history. In his spare time, he enjoys music, films, and writing plays.